KIRK TERREL

AGE OF ARTIFICIAL INTELLIGENCE

The Ultimate Guide To Artificial Intelligence in Digital Marketing, Discover The Ways on How You Can Use Artificial Intelligence to Help Your Business Grow and Succeed

Descrierea CIP a Bibliotecii Naţionale a României
KIRK TERREL
  AGE OF ARTIFICIAL INTELLIGENCE. The Ultimate
Guide To Artificial Intelligence in Digital Marketing, Discover
The Ways on How You Can Use Artificial Intelligence to Help
Your Business Grow and Succeed / Kirk Terrel. – Bucharest:
Editura My Ebook, 2020
  ISBN

KIRK TERREL

AGE OF
ARTIFICIAL INTELLIGENCE

The Ultimate Guide To Artificial Intelligence in Digital Marketing, Discover The Ways on How You Can Use Artificial Intelligence to Help Your Business Grow and Succeed

My Ebook Publishing House
Bucharest, 2020

TABLE OF CONTENTS

INTRODUCTION

Being smart in business means knowing what's just around the corner. It means thinking ahead and preparing for inevitable changes that will impact the way business is conducted. This is what allows a business to be **resilient** and to thrive in a changing environment. Digital marketing is no different.

In fact, in his book *The Personal MBA,* author Josh Kaufman discusses the value of **counterfactual simulation**. This means imagining future possibilities and then preparing for them.

Let's say that you have a big business that is doing well in a specific niche. Maybe you have a company that sells a whey protein shake. The mistake that some big businesses make is to assume that they're too big to fail and to coast along as they are.

But what would happen if another company came along and released a better protein shake for a fraction of the price? What if a new source of protein were to be discovered? What if a study revealed that whey protein was bad for us? Any of these things could happen, and could completely shake up even the most established business.

The *smart* company though, will already have considered these eventualities and prepared for them. THIS is counterfactual simulation: it's thinking about what's just around the corner and then preparing for those possibilities.

As digital marketers, that means thinking about things that could impact on the face of marketing. And one of the things that could have the biggest impact of all? Artificial intelligence.

AI and machine learning have the potential to completely change the face of internet marketing, rendering many older strategies obsolete even. Only by preparing for those changes, can you ensure that your websites manage to hold their position in the SERPs, that your advertising campaigns remain profitable, and that your services remain relevant.

And a lot of this stuff isn't just speculation: it's happening *right now*. AI is already making huge waves even though you might not realize it yet.

It's affecting the way that SEO works, the tools and software we use, and the way that ads are displayed. AI is able to think faster and smarter than any human, and that's especially true when it comes to internet marketing which is a data driven pursuit. An AI marketer can create endless amounts of content in a second – doing the work of hundreds of humans. All of that content will be perfect catered toward the target demographic. AI will run Google. It will manage entire business models. It will run AdWords. And it will run new tools we haven't even dreamed up yet. The digital marketing singularity is just around the corner. This book will help you to prepare, and explain a number of concepts:

- AI vs Machine Learning
- How to conduct SEO now that Google is an "AI first" company
- Chatbots
- Programmatic advertising
- Big data
- RankBrain
- Digital assistants
- Data science
- SQL
- Latent Semantic Indexing
- The future of internet marketing

In this book, you will gain a crystal ball with which to gaze into the future of internet marketing, and to ensure that you are ready for all those changes when they come. By the end, you'll be better prepared and in a better position than 99.9% of other marketers.

CHAPTER 1

WHAT IS AI AND MACHINE LEARNING?

Before we go further, we should first take a look at precisely what AI and machine learning actually are. These are two related but also distinct terms, which often get confused. Both will impact on marketing, but in different and unique ways.

AI then is artificial intelligence. That means software and hardware designed to act and appear intelligent. Such software is capable of making meaningful choices, and conducting activities that we would normally consider the remit of humans.

AI comes in two broad flavors. One is weak AI, which is also known as narrow AI. Weak AI is essentially a form of AI that is designed to perform a *specific* job.

An example of this is the self-driving car. This form of AI is capable of knowing the positions of countless cars on the road, and being able to respond by steering, accelerating, breaking etc. If you were to watch a self-driving car from the outside, you might think a human were driving. In that way, it does a job that would normally be considered a human role.

BUT at the same time, you can't speak with a self-driving car and you can't ask it how it's feeling. A self-driving car would certainly not pass the Turing Test!

Note: The Turing test is a test designed to measure the effectiveness of an AI. If you talk to an AI on a chat app, and you don't know that it isn't human, then it is considered to have "passed the Turing test." Another example of weak AI is used when creating bad guys in computer games. These use programming in order to behave in a human-like manner, and to provide a challenge for the player.

However, the code is only useful in the context of the video game, and so it's not about to turn into Skynet any time soon!

Weak AI might not sound as exciting, but it is being used for a huge range of extremely exciting things – from helping to treat disease, to improving the economy.

Conversely, the type of AI that we often see in science fiction, is what we know as "general AI." This is AI that doesn't have just one purpose, but that is designed to do everything that a human might be able to do. So you could play a word game with this AI, ask it how it's feeling, or get it to look up something useful.

An example of a general AI is DeepMind, owned by Google. DeepMind is a company that has developed a "neural network," that employs "general learning algorithms" to learn a huge range of different skills.

Many AIs such as IBM's Watson are actually pre-programmed. That means that they work using a kind of flow chart, and will answer questions with the same answer every time. On the other hand, DeepMind is apparently able to think and respond via a "convolutional neural network." Certain behaviors and reinforced and encouraged, and these will begin to become more prominent.

This isn't a perfect simulation of how a human brain works (cognitive behavioral psychology teaches us the importance of having internal dialogues and models for thinking), however it is the closest thing we currently have to a "true" general intelligence.

Machine Learning

Machine learning on the other hand works differently. Machine learning utilizes huge data sets in order to gain surprising and almost frightening capabilities at times.

Machine learning essentially allows a piece of software to be "trained." An obvious example of this would be computer vision.

Computer vision describes the ability that some machines have to understand visual information. An example is Google Lens, which can tell you what you're pointing your phone's camera at, whether that's a type of flower, or a product you can buy in stores. Computer vision is necessary for self-driving cars to successfully navigate their environments, and it's used by apps like Snapchat which use filters to change people's faces.

How do these work? By looking at thousands and thousands of pictures of every type of object. While the machine learning algorithm will never understand what it is looking at, it can look for patterns in the data which will then be useful to identify those objects in future. For example, it might notice that faces are typically oval in shape, with a dark patch of hair on top. It then knows that if it sees an oval shape with a dark patch at the top, it's possibly looking at a face.

Machine learning has HUGE potential in just about every field. In future, it can be used to diagnose disease more accurately than a human doctor, to advise on financial decisions, to identify fraudulent bank transfers, and much more.

All of this has HUGE potential implications for internet marketing, and that's what we'll be exploring in the following chapters.

CHAPTER 2

GOOGLE AS AN AI – FIRST COMPANY

A while ago now, Google announced that it had become an AI-first company. While that might sound like meaningless marketing babble, the truth is that this determination actually has HUGE potential repercussions for marketers, businesses, and SEO.

Firstly, what does Google mean by this?

Meet the New, Smarter Google

You might think of Google as a search-first company. The first product that Google provided was a search engine and this is still what most of us associate with the company.

Traditionally, Google's search engine did not work much like an AI. Rather, search worked by attempting to match search terms with the content in an article. This is why the advice for

SEOs was to insert lots of key phrases into their articles, so that Google's spiders could read that content and quickly identify that it would be a good match for what the person was searching for.

As we all know, this didn't work out perfectly for Google. Lots of unscrupulous "marketers" abused the system by inserted hundreds of search terms into every article, which in turn meant the content Google would show to the user would be garbled and unreadable.

That's why, over time, Google has begun to work more and more like an AI. Now, Google no longer attempts to look for exact keyword matches. Instead, Google tries to *answer* questions that you ask it. It does this by trying to understand what the user is looking for along with the context, and then to provide relevant answers through its search.

RankBrain

Google is able to do this through machine learning. Specifically, it uses a form of natural language processing, which Google refers to as RankBrain.

RankBrain is at least partly responsible for helping Google to cope with phrases and words that it hasn't seen before. If

RankBrain identifies a word it isn't familiar with, then it can "guess" what it might mean based on context and based on its usage elsewhere. This helps Google to deal with unusual searches that it hasn't seen before, without simply matching search terms to content in articles.

Search queries are turned into "word vectors", called "distributed representation." These are words and phrases that are close to each other in meaning and context. RankBrain will then try to map the query into words it understands, or clusters of similar words. From there, it insinuates what the searcher actually means and is looking for, and provides results on that basis. RankBrain also understands the relationships *between* words, and the way that they work together.

At one point, joining words such as "the" or "and" were ignored by Google. Now Google understands the importance of these phrases and the way in which they impact on the intent of the user.

Like all the best machine learning algorithms, RankBrain attempts to improve over time and adapt to users. It can see which results get clicked the most and thereby know when it is doing well and when it is getting things wrong. As such, it is able to improve search results for any given keyword quickly through algorithmic testing, which is helping to weed out low quality content that attempts to game the system.

RankBrain works using a **Tensor Processing Unit** (TPU), which is an AI specific piece of hardware stored in Google's data centers. This is a specific chip that is better able to handle the specific challenges of machine learning tasks.

Google's Further Plans

Over the past few years, Google may have seemingly diversified. It now makes smartphones, it now makes self-driving cars, and it now makes apps like Google Lens.

But at the heart of all of these initiatives is some form of AI or machine learning. Google Lens uses machine learning to identify objects in a scene and allow users to that way "search" the real world around them. Self-driving cars of course are highly reliant of various forms of AI.

And the Google Pixel Phones? Arguably, their main focus is putting Google Assistant in everyone's pockets.

And this is the real clue as to what Google is up to. Google Assistant is an AI and virtual assistant that users can use to get weather reports, to book taxis, to play music, and much more. Google Assistant uses a combination of machine learning (to detect human language for example) and AI in order to provide useful results and speak in a natural manner.

Google Assistant is closely integrated with Google search. You can ask Google Assistant a question like "who starred in Iron Man?" and it will give you a natural answer. It does this by first using machine learning to turn your speech into a string, then by using Google Search in order to look up useful answers (which involves machine learning in the form of RankBrain), then by using narrow AI to extract the most useful answers from the best web pages, and then by using another form of narrow AI to provide the response in a natural-sounding manner (which is designed to *appear* like general AI.) Much of this is carried out not on the device that you're speaking to, but on Google's TPUs located in the cloud.

What Does All This Mean for Marketers?

So what does all this mean for marketers? Simple: it means that Google wants to be able to understand your content and extract the most useful information. It no longer wants you to use rigid keywords, and it wants you to prepare for a more voice-driven form of search.

Google is betting big on AI and machine learning. It believes that in the future, AI assistants will be HUGE and it wants Google Assistant to be number one. It envisages a future where we spend less time staring at our devices and instead get the information we need by asking our phones or our Google Homes. We'll speak naturally to these devices, and they'll provide us with handy answers.

CHAPTER 3

PREPARING FOR SEMANTIC SEARCH

Whether Google Assistant eventually becomes the ubiquitous tool that Google wants it to be or not, the fact remains that Google wants search to become increasingly more natural and human. It already has in many ways.

That means that marketers and website owners need to make some changes to the way they do things. It's no longer enough to find a keyword and repeat it a whole lot, you now need to work as though you're speaking with an AI. And that means a couple of things.

LSI: Latent Semantic Indexing

Latent semantic indexing is one of the most important things to consider if you're interested in improving your SEO and getting to the top of Google. It's even *more* critical if you hope to be ready for Google's AI-driven future. Not only is it a powerful concept in itself, but it is also an important microcosm of the broader changes that we are seeing to SEO today.

Search engine optimization is a big and very important part of digital marketing and if you want to drive the maximum number of people to your website or blog then it's absolutely essential that you have the search engines on board.

In the past, SEO has largely relied on creating tons of content around a certain topic and repeatedly using a set number of keywords or key phrases in that content in order to help Google identify the subject and help the right visitors to find your pages. Unfortunately, a few people began to take advantage of this system and began 'keyword stuffing' by using the same keywords over and over again to the point of distraction. Google had to get smarter and so it did.

Today, using the same keyword too much will get you into trouble. So what does Google do instead? It looks at context and the broader subject of the article. In other words, it looks for synonyms and related terms and this *also* gives it the ability to better understand what your page is about.

For instance, if you had written an article about "decision trees," then in the past Google could theoretically have gotten confused and brought your site up as a result when someone searched for trees. It may have thought you were talking about decisions *about* trees!

Now though, it can look for related terms like "flow chart" and thus help to more accurately match article to reader. LSI actually comes from mathematics, and uses a technique called singular value decomposition. This means that it will scan unstructured data and look for the relationships between the words and concepts within.

How to Handle LSI

So how do you make sure your site is LSI optimized? Short answer: you don't.

While it is obviously tempting for SEO companies to now start offering their LSI optimized services, the truth is that you should have been doing this *all along* and without thinking about it. That's what the best web marketers like Andrej Ilisin have always recommended and its what Matt Cutts advises as well.

In short, writing naturally *should* mean that you are including synonyms and related topics. Otherwise your writing is going to sound pretty repetitive. The moral is what it's always been: stop double guessing and just write for the reader! This is something we'll come back to again and again with regards to preparing for a smarter Google.

But there are also some other tips you can keep in mind if you want to ensure that Google knows what you're talking about.

First, make sure that you use more than one search phrase. It's a good idea for a whole host of reasons to use a combination of different search terms, rather than targeting just a single one. Seeing as Google will often show results that don't use the exact key phrase the person searched for, it makes sense to try and include a few popular iterations of the same term.

Likewise, you should make sure to use good and varied vocabulary around the topic. This helps to better demonstrate the context and the subject matter of your article. Rather than filling an article with random synonyms, think instead about words that would often occur alongside the topic you're working with (such as our earlier example of flow charts.) This is called co-occurrence, and it's the kind of thing that machine learning algorithms love!

Structured Data

The other big concept that SEOs need to consider in order to be ready for the AI Google of the future, is schema markups, also known as structured data, also known as rich data.

Remember: Google's aim is to enable Assistant to answer natural language question with useful responses, which will draw on information found on the web. Google doesn't just want to pull up a list of useful search results, it wants to be able to answer questions. So if someone asks how to make bolognaise, it will simply read out the ingredients.

In order to do this, Google needs to be able to find that most relevant information in a passage of text, and then pull out the specific answer. This takes the concept of RankBrain to the next level, allowing it to understand not just what an article is about, but how each *paragraph* in that article functions.

The problem is that Google's AI can't quite do this yet. At least not well enough to be able to usefully provide answers for people without occasionally including completely nonsense!

That's where schema markups come in.

The idea of a schema markup, is to essentially annotate your articles and blog posts by telling Google what each bit is and what it does. Essentially, you are saying "this is a list of ingredients" or "this is a user rating."

This also helps Google to provide what are known as "rich snippets." Rich snippets are search results on the SERPs (Search Engine Results Pages) that include more than just a meta description. You might see a search result listed for instance that also includes bullet point steps, or that includes ingredients for the meal. This way, the user can see the information they're looking for without even needing to leave that website!

How to Use Markups

Markups look a lot like HTML. Here's an example of what this might look like:

```
<DIV ITEMSCOPE
ITEMTYPE="HTTP://SCHEMA.ORG/LOCALBUSINESS">
<A ITEMPROP="URL" HREF="HTTP://WWW.FIREFLY-
FLORAL.COM"><DIV
ITEMPROP="NAME"><STRONG>THE CANDLE
FACTORY</STRONG></DIV>
</A>
<DIV ITEMSCOPE
ITEMTYPE="HTTP://SCHEMA.ORG/ORGANIZATION">
```

```
<SPAN ITEMPROP="TELEPHONE">888-888-8888</SPAN>
</DIV>
```

That is basically telling Google that you are talking about a local business (The Candle Factory). You can also use schema to highlight product names, authors, aggregate ratings, software applications, restaurants, movies, and much more!

To use this yourself, you can either look up the HTML code and implement it yourself, or you can use Google's handy markup helper: https://www.google.com/webmasters/markup-helper/u/0/.

Here, you will simply share the URL of the page you want to markup, and it will then provide you with the opportunity to create the necessary tags.

There are also plugins you can use to the same end through WordPress.

The Good and the Bad of Schema Markups

The savvy among you may have noticed some worrying issues with schema markups. Specifically: they encourage people *not* to visit your website!

Let's say you have a recipes website, and you included an article on cooking bolognaise. You probably did this, hoping that people would search for it on Google, find your website, and then visit your page in order to read about it. In doing so, they might also click on a few ads, they might buy an affiliate product, or they might just remember your brand so that they come back again in future.

But if Google simply takes your key information and shares it, then there is no real incentive for them to actually visit your webpage. As such, there is no chance they will click on your ads, or buy your products. They'll not even know that the information *came* from your website!

Essentially, Google is this way using our intellectual property without any remuneration – which has upset a lot of webmasters, businesses, and marketers.

So should you avoid using these features altogether? Unfortunately, that is not really an option. Remember, Google *also* uses markups in order to provide rich snippets. These are the more media-rich search listings which include things like star ratings, images, bullet points, and more. These really help a webpage to stand out in the SERPs, and thereby ensure that more people click on that listing.

And while you might not get any benefit from having Google read your ingredients out, if you don't include markup language, then it will just get that same information from one of your competitors. Google wants us to use schema markups, and that means that it will likely reward those sites that do with a little SEO boost. For all those reasons, it's essential that you keep using this strategy *even though* you might be giving Google free information in doing so.

In future, if more and more people talk to their Google Assistant rather than browsing the web for information, then there's a chance Google might need to rethink its policy: lest it face a rather big backlash from content creators!

CHAPTER 4
BIG DATA

You might hear the term "big data" thrown around a lot and not fully understand what is meant by it. In this chapter, you will be enlightened and learn how big data can help you and your business, both now and in the future.

Essentially, big data is nothing more than *large data sets*. These large data sets are increasingly common online, seeing as everything online is easy to measure and document. If you think about a company like Google, it has *immense* data sets that it works from, describing the search history of billions of users.

But even a standard website that gets 1,000 visitors a day will work with huge amounts of information. A website will naturally record each of those visits and will also store data about each one – such as the country of origin, and the length of time spent on the site. In a few weeks, this data will likely crash a lot of spreadsheet software!

The reason that big data is featured in so many discussions is that it is very difficult to handle. Making sense of such huge amounts of information requires a lot of smart math, while simply storing and handling that kind of data requires a lot of storage and computational power.

But the potential value of big data is also absolutely huge. Big data provides patterns and insights that you simply can't get by observing a few users. This is essentially how machine learning works – by looking for patterns in massive data sets. The difference is that this is being leveraged in a slightly different way.

Predictive Modelling

Predictive modelling is a process that involves data mining and probability to forecast potential future outcomes. A model is created using a number of "predictors." Predictors are variables that are thought to influence future results.

Once data is collected for those predictors, a statistical model can be created. That might use a simple linear equation, or it might use complex neural networks. Either way, statistical analysis can then be used in order to make predictions about how things are likely to go in future.

With regards to marketing, this can help provide better customer insights, better lead scoring, campaign nurturing, upselling and cross-selling, personalized product recommendations and more!

Amazon is an example of a site that uses big data in order to provide personalized product recommendations. Amazon doesn't just use a database of items grouped together (which would be almost impossible to maintain) but rather generates data automatically from every single transaction and sale, and then looks for patterns. It will see what products tend to be bought together (there's that co-occurrence again) and can therefore use this information to show items that it thinks a user might want to buy next!

Likewise, when it comes to lead scoring, big data can be immensely useful. Lead scoring means understanding which leads are likely ready to purchase and which are not. This is immensely useful information for companies that might want to send sales letters to the cross section of their mailing list that they think will actually buy from them (rather than being put off by the amount of sales material they're receiving).

Amnesty International uses segmentation and "predictive modelling" techniques in order to better identify the right groups to market toward. By collecting data and then looking at what that data reveals about the kinds of people who donate, Amnesty International knows who it should be targeting with its ads, how much they are likely to spend, and how they're likely to do it.

Any charity can benefit from this kind of data analysis, as can any business.

Collecting Big Data

If you want to start collecting data for your business, there are a wide number of plugins and tools you can use to do so. You should find that a lot of tools, such as Google Analytics, will allow you to export massive amounts of data in order to work on.

You can then choose to use this information yourself, or to outsource it to a data science organization that can use that information to provide valuable, useful insights.

Another good idea to prepare yourself for the future, is to allow users to create profiles. By doing this, you can collect much more data on individual users, and in future provide better recommendations on an individual basis too. This is something that stores have been doing for decades with loyalty cards, but of course the digital nature of selling online creates even more potential opportunities!

CHAPTER 5

COMPUTER VISION

As mentioned, computer vision is the ability for machines and computers to "see" by learning from huge data sets and machine learning. By observing countless images, a machine can learn to identify images in an object, or to navigate an environment without crashing into things.

What does this mean for the future of SEO?

One BIG thing – and one thing that you should make sure that you are ready for – is that Google will likely start paying more attention to images on websites.

Traditionally, we have been told to avoid using images for things like site names. Why? Because Google can't "read" and image, and therefore we won't get any SEO benefit from that.

But Google does have software that can read text from an image. This is called OCR (Optical Character Recognition) and if you want to see just how good it is, try pointing Google Translate at a foreign language and see it appear in your native tongue in real time. If Google can do this, then it's only a matter of time before it starts reading the text in your images to see if they back up the niche and keyphrase that you are targeting with your website.

Likewise, seeing as facial recognition is already a big deal when it comes to security and Facebook, it is probably only a matter of time before Google starts using that too.

For example, if you write a blog post about Sylvester Stallone, Google might someday look not only at your content, but also at the photos on your page in order to see if there are pictures of Stallone there! Google Images might one day not be reliant on surrounding text at all, but might instead base its results purely on what it sees in the image, and whether this lines up with what you're searching for.

Issues like image *quality* are also likely to play a big role in future. Google might opt not to recommend your webpage if it thinks the imagery on there is poorly chosen and out of place.

So what can you do to prepare? For now, the closest thing to communicating with Google via images is the use of markup language and/or file names and alt tags. Using alt tags to describe images can help Google to know what they represent, and therefore to better decide if your site is relevant for a particular user.

Meanwhile, make sure that all the imagery you are using is relevant and high quality!

CHAPTER 6
ADVERTISING

At its core, machine learning is about evolving. It's about getting more and more data, to the point that it can make more accurate assertions. While face detection in images might start out poor, the system evolves and learns to the point where it becomes more accurate than a human.

Imagine if you could turn that power to advertising. Imagine if you could show precisely right advertisements, to precisely the right people, at precisely the right times. Imagine if your advertising campaign "evolved" to get more and more specific, so that an increasingly large number of viewers clicked on the ads and bought your products. The longer the campaign ran, the more your profits would increase and the less you'd spend on ineffectual ads.

That is precisely how programmatic advertising works, and you can start using it right now!

What is Programmatic Advertising?

Programmatic advertising campaigns allow marketers to buy native ads on a variety of publisher's sites while using smart algorithms to ensure that they are targeting the right viewers at the right times all while remaining within budget thanks to a bidding system that allows them to compete for impressions with other advertisers.

In short these campaigns give the precision and quality of native advertising (like banner ads) while at the same time allowing for the control, adaptability and precision that you would get with a PPC campaign. The net result is ads appearing on the sites of carefully selected publishers, but only when and if they are likely to yield the best results.

Programmatic advertising uses a complex algorithm in order to identify your business' ideal customer, and then to figure out where they are likely to appear on the web. It will then show the ads in those places and then utilize a learning algorithm to

Instead of going from one publisher to another discussing rates, you allow a "bot" to do all the work for you. More importantly though, this means that you won't waste money on an ad slot that no one looks at. Your ads will be chosen and honed by a smart algorithm, and the result will be that they get higher CTRs from the right targeted customers!

RTB

This is how programmatic buying is different from either PPC or just buying a banner ad on your favourite news site. Giving you further control meanwhile is the option to use RTB or "Real Time Bidding."

What RTB essentially means is that you are automatically entering into a bidding war each time a page loads based on your pre-defined budget. These bidding wars allow your ads to compete with other advertisers around a large selection of different websites that all cater to the specific demographics and context that you have chosen. In other words, you will define that you want to target sports sites catering to an audience of males in their 20s-40s, and from there your ads will appear across a selection of those websites (which you can still curate in some cases if you wish) based on the outcome of each little bid. This allows you to target your audience across a range of different sites and to avoid paying too much to do so).

On the other hand, direct buying is essentially a bulk order of impressions from a specific website/website(s) such as ESPN. You can still filter your impressions by a range of factors such as location or browser, but essentially you will be targeting a specific site and securing a place on that precise spot.

Direct buying is effectively a little more like advertising with a banner ad, while RTB is a little closer to the PPC model here you bid for spots across a range of websites (while still having a little more control).

Deciding what will work best for you will depend on a number of factors. For instance, your budget is going to come into play as direct buying tends to be more expensive (because lower CPIs won't have as many opportunities to appear). It's also worth considering that RTB gives you more flexibility, more data and more control – you can identify which sites are working best for you, at which times and for which viewers, and then you can further tailor your approach accordingly.

On the other hand though, if you bid *too* low using RTB, then you risk your ads not appearing at all. This is in direct contrast to direct buys which essentially "guarantee" you your ad spot and that you will eventually be certain to get that number of impressions. This is useful for a company with more concrete goals and a fixed timescale. Likewise, with direct buying you will be able to more tightly control where your advertising appears and forge a closer relationship between your brand and that of the publisher.

So different approaches will work for different marketers and for different purposes. Your job is to decide which works best for you, and the best way to do that may well be to dip your toe in and try them out for yourself.

How to be More Successful With Programmatic Buying

Programmatic advertising has very quickly risen to prominence in the online marketing industry and is an important new tool for any business that wants to reach a bigger audience. That said though, even the best programmatic tools are only as effective as the people controlling them, so before you get ahead of yourself consider these four crucial tips to ensure your success.

Don't Forget the Creative Component

No matter how well targeted your ads are or how smart your campaign is in terms of exposure, if you haven't invested in the creative aspect then those ads are going to fall flat. Design your ads well and test to see which designs work best. Likewise, think about your brand identity and how you can strengthen this even through ads that don't get clicked. Choose a programmatic partner who can help you with this aspect.

Consider Audience and Context

Before choosing which publishers to work with you need to look at the audience they are attracting *as well* as the context. The ideal partner will be a site that writes about topics related to yours and targets the precise same demographic you are.

In some cases though you won't be able to find both, and thus you will need to select publishers that provide the best balance. And don't be tempted to ignore context in these situations, because studies show that the same person is far more likely to click on an ad for golf clubs when they're on a golfing website compared with a news site. More to the point, someone who wants a wedding dress is *only* going to want that wedding dress during a particular time in their life and this really demonstrates the importance of context.

Be Willing to Spend to Begin With

The beauty of programmatic advertising is that you can directly manage your spending in real time to ensure you get the maximum exposure whatever your budget. However, it's highly recommended that you start out with a higher spending-limit than you intend to continue with, as this will enable you to more quickly identify what works and what doesn't. Remember, you want more *data* and that means you want more clicks. As you tweak your campaign in response to stats and ROI you will get closer and closer to the optimum set-up, but if you don't spend the money up front then you won't be able to tell if your campaign is working because you won't win enough bids. Spend a little up front and you'll save money in the long run once you settle into your groove.

Make Sure Your Ads Fit In

The downside of any automated advertising campaign is that you can lose that "personal touch" – the benefits that come from working with a publisher to develop an advertising campaign that matches the tone and appearance of their overall site and that they will help to promote throughout their content.

Unfortunately, native advertising is difficult to scale which is why so many automatic platforms are popular.

To be successful with programmatic advertising this is something you need to consider. Your ad is targeting the right people, on the right devices in the right contexts. But is it the right fit for the job? This ad needs to look like a native ad in the same way that a banner ad would. Creating ads that will blend into a number of "environments" is one way to do this. Another is to choose a tool that allows you to select the brands you want to work with, and then to choose those that are *already* closely aligned with your own goals and style.

CHAPTER 7

EMAIL MARKETING

The key to success on the web is not just to *gain* traffic but also to control that traffic. What does that mean? It means that you need to know how to decide which of your visitors you want to talk to at any time. It means that you need to understand your visitors and to know what they're thinking, what their moods are and what they're interested in at any given time. And it means you need to know how and when to strike when it comes to selling products or encouraging people to sign up to your mailing list. This is a theme we've seen come up time and again with machine learning and AI. And email marketing is no different.

You can do all this by building a mailing list and then *segmenting* that list.

First, let's go over the basics of email marketing again for those that aren't familiar.

Email marketing is of course the process of marketing via email. In other words, this means you're going to be building a big list – a collection of emails – and you'll do this by asking visitor to your site to share their contact details when they land on your home page.

This in turn requires an autoresponder. An autoresponder is a tool that you use to create email forms and then to manage all of the contacts on your list. You can use the form somewhere on your page to let people input their details and you'll use the autoresponder to actually send all your emails.

It should be immediately apparent what the value of this is. Sending all your emails manually using Gmail or another web client is not easy and would likely result in many not getting delivered. You'd have to send lots of different emails for longer lists and you'd need to manually manage any requests to subscribe or unsubscribe.

An autoresponder manages all that for you, so you just need to write one email and then click "send." The other benefit of an autoresponder though is that it can collect data for you and use that information to do a range of different things. For example, an autoresponder can show you the percentage of subscribers who actually open your emails. If your email subject headings aren't successfully encouraging people to read, then you can identify this problem and work on a solution.

Suddenly, we're using a data-driven approach and machine learning again!

You can then see all the visitors who *did* read a given message in one place. Or choose to see all the ones that didn't. You can see the open rate for different individual visitors and you organize your list by different factors.

That's another handy thing about using an autoresponder: it will allow you to grab more information using the form embedded on your page and that information can then be used to group your visitors. Want to just message the men? Go for it. Want to just message the people over 30? You can do that too. Or how about having multiple different mailing lists for different brands, or even for different products? All of this can be accomplished using just a single autoresponder.

And of course, this kind of control and automation opens up all sorts of possibilities when it comes to AI and machine learning for marketers.

Lead Warmth and Email Segmentation

The true power of all this information comes from being able to use it that data in order to pick and choose who your messages go to. For instance, you can decide that you want to send an email only to people who fall into particular categories.

What we're interested in to begin with is sending emails based on engagement, retention and lead warmth.

A lead is anyone who has shown some kind of interest in buying from you. That means that anyone who has signed up to your mailing list can be considered a lead because they have demonstrated an interest simply by doing this.

But at the same time, a lead is also anyone who visits your site, or who takes your card. This is a 'cold' lead, whereas someone who actually gives you their contact details is a 'warm' lead.

Leads get warmer the more interest they show in what you do and what you're selling. And the warmer a lead is, the more likely they are to buy from you.

In fact, this is the true and most useful purpose of *having* a mailing list to begin with: it allows you to take your ice cold leads and turn them into warm leads and then paying customers.

I always liken this to asking for someone's phone number. If you were to just walk up to someone in a club and ask for their number, they'd likely just tell you to go away.

Why would they give you their number when they know nothing about you and have shown no interest in you?

First, you need to chat to them and let them get to know you. If they look at you and smile, they're a cold lead. If they respond to your witty banter and tell you their name, they're a warm lead. If they've kissed you or let you buy them a drink, they're a hot lead. And once they're hot, you can ask for their number.

This is all about timing. Time this wrong and they're not going to give you their number because you haven't laid the ground work!

The exact same thing is true with internet marketing. If someone visits your site and you tell them right away to buy your product, they won't. Why would they? You haven't given them any reason to trust you. You haven't told them anything about you. They don't know much about the product.

Ask them to hand over their email after a few blog posts though and you can gently start to increase engagement. This is then when you wow them with all your information and all your knowledge. You entertain them a little and you let them get to know you.

If they don't open your emails, that's the equivalent of giving you the cold shoulder. That's like the girl or guy in the club that isn't laughing at your jokes and keeps looking away. If you try and sell to them now, you become spam. And you get deleted.

And they never return to your website.

But if they open your emails, you know you're in with a shot. That means you can then send them some more information about your products and get them excited for your product launch. If during that they *still* keep opening your emails, then you know you've got an even better chance of success. If you now try and sell to them, there's a *much* better chance they'll buy from you.

Using email segmentation you can do exactly that: you can see which of your visitors are actually opening your emails, are actually clicking your links and are scrolling down to the bottom.

In fact, using cookies it is even possible to see which of those visitors has been to your website and looked at your products. You can see who has hovered on your products and been tempted to click buy.

Email Segmentation Combined With Machine Learning

If you've been paying close attention, then you might already have figured out where this is going. Remember when we discussed big data, we said that you could use predictive analytics in order to better rate leads?

This is where things could get really interested for the autoresponders of the future. Imagine if your autoresponder not only segmented your audience and looked at the open rates and engagement, but if it could look for trends across huge data sets.

In other words, what if your autoresponder recorded every single person who bought from you, and assess what actions they usually *took first*. This would allow that machine learning algorithm to better spot when a user is behaving like someone ready to buy, and to send them a message tailored to encourage that purchase!

This could be combined with smart recommendations in order to improve their likelihood of buying even more.

This is already being used by some big brands, so it's only a matter of time until more of us get access to this same amount of precision.

Tips Marketers Can Follow Now

For *any* of that to work, you also need to make sure that people are signing up to your mailing list in the first place. Again, this will help us to prepare for the AI-powered future. There are a few ways you can encourage this.

Firstly, make sure that you show your mailing list wherever you can. At the very least, that should mean that your mailing list shown at the bottom of your posts. At the same time though, you can also place this in the side bars so that your list is visible on every page of your site.

Another tip is to make sure that you draw attention to it. A mistake a lot of people make is to create their mailing list and then just 'hope' that people see it. Far more effective is to occasionally tell people about it and to explain in your posts why it's a good opportunity and why people should be excited to sign up.

Here's the thing though: you should *always* be honest.

The aim of a mailing list is not to grow it as much as you possibly can. Instead, the aim is to grow it as much as you can with only *highly targeted* visitors.

If your visitors have no interest in what you're offering through your list, then you will just frustrate them and effectively be spamming.

CHAPTER 8

CHATBOTS

Chatbots are an increasingly popular tool for marketers, business owners, and webmasters. So what is a chatbot?

Essentially, a chatbot is a miniscule AI that will normally live on a website, and which will then be able to answer questions and engage in basic conversation.

Very often, chatbots are used in customer service. This way, a website can answer commonly asked questions and significantly lighten the load on its customer service team. The company can provide the support it wants to for its buyers, without spending a huge amount on extra members of staff and call centers.

But a chatbot can be much more than just customer support. Chatbots are just as effective in marketing, and can be extremely effective at increasing sales and profits. Chatbots are particularly effective at kickstarting a sales process, by welcoming visitors to a website and asking them what they're looking for. Instead of relying on UX to try and guide the visitor to the right part of the page, a chatbot can instead simply *ask* what they are hoping to buy, and then take them to that page. What's more is that it can provide useful recommendations (perhaps informed by previous buying history) and it can reduce any concerns that users might have.

Chatbots can even get information from customers, by asking them their budget, or what it is they're looking for. Even if they don't buy, you now understand their intent and you can use this information to hone your marketing strategy further.

Some pundits argue that in the next few years, 85% of business might be done through chatbots! So how can you get started? 80% of businesses say they want chatbots in place by 2020!

Facebook Chatbots

One option is to invest in a Facebook chatbot. There are plenty of sites and services online that will set these up for you.

Facebook Messenger is a new frontier for a lot of small businesses. While it has crept under the radar for many marketers, the numbers speak for themselves. Facebook

Messenger is currently used by over 1.2 billion people! That's 11% of the *entire human population.*

And what makes Messenger even more powerful, is that it can be embedded into your website. Over 20 million pages use messaging and that number is growing. This provides a very simple and easy way to communicate with your visitors, to answer their queries and to help convert traffic into sales.

But you can't be available 24/7 to cater to all your visitors' needs. And this is where a chatbot comes in. This is a basic AI that can tend to your customers and help to provide a more personal experience while answering basic questions.

This is a *hugely* powerful tool for businesses as it means you'll no longer lose visitors that struggled to find their way around the website or to get the information they need.

Imagine if customers could order food by just sending a Facebook message and then answering a few automated questions?

Or what if a business could access your expert legal advice without ever needing to speak to you in person? All of this is possible in the near future.

Facebook chatbots can even be *proactive* by sending messages to potential customers. You need to be extremely careful with this, seeing as it can be seen as spam. But if you have an automated system that's able to reach out to potential buyers at just the right time with a carefully crafted message, this can be huge for business!

Other Types of Chatbot

Of course, not all chatbots are Facebook chatbots. There are many other ways to implement chatbots into a website, from creating them from scratch using home-made software, to using them to respond to emails or SMS.

CHAPTER 9

DEVELOPING YOUR AI SKILLS – USING SQL

If you want to ensure you aren't left behind by developments in AI and machine learning, then it may pay to learn relevant skills that you can use to implement your own strategies. At least by understanding the tools used in AI and machine learning, you will be able to navigate these new horizons and make smarter decisions for your business.

One of the key concepts to understand then is SQL. SQL stands for Structured Query Language, and is a declarative language that is used to store and retrieve information from a database. If that sounds like gobbledygook, it basically provides a set of commands you can use to manipulate large data sets.

SQL is crucial for data science and machine learning. It takes a number of forms such as MySQL, SQL Server, and SQLite. Each uses a slightly different dialect to achieve the same thing: interact with relational databases.

Relational databases consist of numerous tables like you see in Excel, with columns and rows. So if you had a list of visitors to your website, you might fill out their data across rows, such as name, age, contact details, etc. Pull out any given visitor, and it will bring their details up so that you're ready to call them and market to them.

SQL then allows you to do things like creating whole new tables, or inserting new rows, columns, or cells. You can do this with simple commands like "CREATE TABLE" and "INSERT INTO."

To make a new database, you first need to use a command to make it, and from there you can then begin inserting tables like so:

```
CREATE TABLE CLIENTS (
ROWID INTEGER PRIMARY KEY, LASTNAME TEXT,
FIRSTNAME TEXT, PHONE TEXT, EMAIL TEXT
);
```

One of the more powerful commands is something called SELECT which will allow you to retrieve information across one or more tables. For instance, you can use this to get the details of anyone over a certain age, like so:

SELECT FIRSTNAME FROM CLIENTS WHERE AGE > 23;

GROUP BY is a command that lets you group results according to certain conditions. CURSORS let us move through sets of data and make changes.

While this all might seem quite simple, combined with huge amounts of data, these simple commands can yield fascinating results and be extremely useful in informing future decisions. This is essentially how machine learning works, and if ever you want to work as a data scientist to employ big data solutions or machine learning applications, this is what you will need to know.

CHAPTER 10

HOW TO FUTURE PROOF YOUR MARKRTING

Over the course of this ebook, we've examined a large number of different types of AI and machine learning in the context of digital marketing.

The objective of all of this has been to help you better prepare for the future. You know that you should start collecting as much data as possible right now, that you need to add schema markups to your site, that you should be using LSI, that you could benefit from a chatbot…

You even know a little bit about SQL, just in case you ever decide to get involved behind the scenes! But in all likelihood, all of this is going to change a lot more before it enters the scene – and we can't really anticipate just how its impact will be felt.

There are huge waves making their way through internet marketing, and the power of AI can't really be understated. Imagine for instance, what will happen once AI that can write high quality content becomes commonplace and commercially available. This technology already exists – AI that can write nearly as well as a human – but when it is allowed to cut loose on the web, it could potentially flood the internet with enough new content to double or triple its size in a matter of days!

How will we know what's written by a human and what's not? What about when AI can create realistic looking images? We've already seen the power of deep fakes: how will we know what's real and what's not?

We can't really prepare for these scenarios because we don't know how they will play out. So for now, it is best to focus on what we *do* know. And in particular, as a marketer, that means focussing on Google's move to natural language processing and more human-like interactions.

It also means that Google is going to keep getting smarter. Google used to look for keyword matches, but now it actually understands the meaning of a website and can use many more metrics in order to understand whether it is high or low quality, and whether it is delivering on what it claims to do.

In fact, Google likely has the potential to become the most powerful AI on the planet, owing to the huge amount of information it has access to, and the huge resources that the company pour into it. This makes it increasingly difficult to 'game' the system or to try and trick Google.

The best thing we can do then? Make the best quality content we can. As Google becomes more and more human, writing for Google and writing for the reader will mean essentially the same thing. It's time we started focussing on great quality content, and on providing real value.

The key thing to remember is that Google serves its customers first and foremost. Who are its customers? The users who use it to find information and entertainment. Google wants people to keep using its search, and as such, it needs to make sure it consistently brings up only the most relevant and interesting information.

As long as you are concerned with creating great quality content for your readers, then your goals and Google's will be aligned. Thus, each time it gets a little bit smarter, that will work to your favour instead of being something you need to worry about.

As Google gets smarter, it will find *more* ways of identifying the best quality content. And so if you're focussed on delivering that, Google will find more ways of connecting you with your audience.

Combine this with more data collection, and a generally more data-driven approach to marketing, and you will be ready for the future of the industry.

Printed by Libri Plureos GmbH in Hamburg,
Germany